Losing

a pet

WHAT READERS SAY...

"From the practicalities, right through to the profound emotional impact that losing a beloved companion can have on us, Jane shows such empathy and insight into every aspect of pet loss. I will be recommending this book to all of our clients." **Ally Todd-McCabe, Pet Funeral Director, Trusted Friends**

"I lost my cat companion of 12 years yesterday in an emotional farewell at the vets. Reading your book today has helped me greatly, helped me to normalise what I am experiencing and brought me a great deal of ease at a time where my heart feels broken." **Phil**

"Your book gave me permission to feel what I was feeling, including the numbness, which was very unnerving and guilt-inducing until I read your book." **Donna**

"I was given this book in 2010 by a pet crematorium where I had taken my dearly beloved dog of ten years. I was heartbroken at the time, but those around me, as do many who do not have animals, carried on rather normally - this book brought me the comfort when they could not. I have since bought this book for friends who have lost their pets, and each one of them has said it has helped them and they wish they knew about it before." **Ripley**

Losing
A Pet

Coping with the death of your beloved animal

Jane Matthews

First published in Great Britain in 2007 by small books

This revised and updated edition published in 2019

A CIP catalogue record for this book is available from the British Library

ISBN: 978-0-9556643-2-8

small books
21 Station Terrace
Great Linford
Milton Keynes MK14 5AP

About the author

Jane Matthews writes books and leads workshops on living more authentically, creating better relationships, building self-esteem and healing from the past. Her latest titles include *The Carer's Handbook* (3ʳᵈ edition, Robinson 2019), and *Have the Best Year of Your Life* (o books 2010).

Jane is an accredited teacher of Louise Hay's *Heal Your Life®* programmes and has been leading workshops and working with individuals since 2006. She works in both the UK and on behalf of Serenity Retreat (www.serenityretreat.co.uk) in Greece.

She has worked as a features journalist on local, national and specialist titles, winning awards for campaigns on homelessness and social justice.

DEDICATION

For Amy and Paul, who have shared with me the joy our beloved pets bring into our homes and lives.

Paul and Twiglet

CONTENTS

Chapter 1

Living with a Pet

Our pets are what turn our houses into homes.

Whenever I've been away, whether it's for a few hours or for a long holiday, it's my cats I look forward to seeing again; more than the bricks and mortar, or the garden or the letters on the mat.

At the end of the day, when I collapse in the chair with a cup of tea and my thoughts, it's my pets I want alongside: easy, companionable, happy to let me be me.

And when I'm upset, it's they who instinctively know to come and offer comfort and quiet company.

AN OPEN HEART IS A VULNERABLE HEART

But the moment we choose to keep a pet we make ourselves vulnerable by laying our hearts on the line. Even if our cat or dog or pony or rabbit lives to an old age then the chances are we'll still live longer.

Sadly, many of them don't live out their full lifespan, but are taken early from us by illness, or in accidents. Or they simply disappear and we never know where or why.

We know our pets are not people, but that doesn't stop our hearts breaking when we lose them.

Losing a pet can be every bit as devastating, every bit as traumatic, as any other bereavement.

SUFFERING IN SILENCE

Because such losses are rarely written or talked about, we are often unsure whether to share them, not trusting others to understand the depth of our pain. Instead, we suffer in silence.

The one thing in our life that has always been there for us when we are grieving is the very reason we are inconsolable. Without any obvious outlet for our pain, it can feel as if it is almost too much to bear.

"The hardest part for me was knowing that others wouldn't understand. I knew people would be thinking "it's just a rabbit" so to think I was grieving so heavily would seem ridiculous to some. It made it harder for me to address the grief around others, which contributed to why I grieved for such a long time." **Sally**

A TALE OF FIVE CATS

Most animal lovers suspect that it is their pets who chose them rather than the other way around. That was certainly true for us when one Saturday morning someone rang the doorbell and ran away.

The doormat wasn't quite empty. There at our feet was a battered cardboard box and nestled inside were a mother cat and her four kittens.

The mother was a shorthaired tabby, painfully thin. Her eyes looked hollow and sad - in contrast to her kittens, whose eyes were still tightly shut to this new world they'd suddenly arrived in.

Two of the kittens were long-haired tabbies, sooty furballs curled into each other. The third had short hair like its mother, only several shades of smoke lighter. The fourth kitten was the colour of an apricot, its long hair curling from its soft belly. To this day we have no idea who brought the cats, nor why they chose our entirely ordinary, terraced house.

But what a wonderful favour they did us.

Princess – named by the children – and her small brood dug themselves into the house, into the furniture, and into our hearts.

By the time two months had passed and, with it, the date the RSPCA told us the kittens would be weaned and they could take them off our hands, we were besotted – and determined to find a way of ensuring we could still see the little creatures who had snuffled, poked and purred their way into our lives.

The little apricot cat, now called Marmalade, went to our babysitter, while the light tabby, who'd inherited his mother's watchful eyes, went to an uncle who named him Scrumpy.

We called the two long-haired kittens Pocket and Tails and found a willing home for the male, Tails, with an aunt. Pocket, we decided, should stay with her mother – and with us.

LOVE AND LOSS

Just like your pets, ours brought us so much joy, fun and loving companionship over the years. They were part of the family and so, so easy to love and enjoy.

When my uncle died, it was an obvious thing to do to bring home again the little tabby we'd boarded out to him. Scrumpy may not have been a favourite with his mother and sister, who clearly resented having to share us with an interloper, but we loved having him back in the family fold.

Thirteen years have passed since they arrived. Two years ago we lost Princess, most likely to a car. She managed to make it home but died of internal injuries according to the vet.

And now Pocket has joined her. Our dear, irrepressible Pocket, so full of character and love it seemed such a small body could hardly contain all that living.

Pocket, too, died as a result of a car. Too many people travelling too far and too fast: the precise opposite of our pets whose whole presence serves to slow us down, relax us, and remind us that however mad the world might sometimes seem, it is affection and friendship, the deep peace that comes from loving and being loved, that makes life worthwhile.

That turns our houses into homes.

HOW I CAME TO WRITE THIS BOOK
It was losing little Pocket that led me to write this book.

Like you, probably, I had experienced loss before. I cried when my grandparents died and wept for my uncle, even though I knew his death was a release from the pain of cancer.

But I was unprepared for the depth of my grief at the loss of that small cat. I remember sitting alongside her silent body for hours, stroking her fur, utterly bereft.

I felt empty, guilty, awkward, lost. How could I possibly go into work, red-eyed and ready to weep the moment anyone said a kind word to me? Surely it was wrong or unnatural to feel so strongly about losing a pet? I couldn't imagine sharing those feelings with friends or colleagues for fear they or I would find the depth of my grief embarrassing.

How could I be grieving for an animal in a way I never had for my own relatives? And how could I explain the fact that I was still so sad weeks, even months after her untimely death?

Sitting down and writing about my feelings, trying to make sense of them, helped ease the pain a little. It also – in time – gave me the opportunity to speak to many others who knew exactly how I felt. Because they'd experienced all of those troubling – and sometimes overpowering – emotions too.

If there can ever be an upside to death then losing dear Pocket gave me a chance to understand that actually there is nothing wrong or unusual about grieving so hard and so long for a beloved pet. And then to decide to set down for others the things that worked for me as, slowly, I healed from her loss.

I knew I wanted the book to be short and to the point; available as a kind of first aid for anyone facing the loss of a beloved animal.

Though I'd already had a number of books published I decided I'd publish this one myself, mainly because the size and content didn't fit neatly into any publishers' portfolio and I wanted the book to be affordable – costing not much more than a sympathy card.

Over the years since *Losing a Pet* first appeared it's been sold and given away in vet surgeries and pet crematoria and it's been studied as part of a course for animal health professionals.

But above all it's been sold or given to individuals, many of whom I've heard from, by letter or over the phone, and whose own experiences now appear in this new edition.

YOU AND YOUR BELOVED PET

If you are reading this because your pet has died I am so very, very sorry for your loss. And I know that, at this moment, it may feel as if the grief will never end; that you will never be able to remember the good times you shared without every memory bringing you right back to your sadness.

In your grief may you find some comfort in this short book; in the experiences of others who may not have known your wonderful companion but know something of what you are going through.

In the recognition that this is *not* a small loss and that there is nothing unusual or wrong about the depth of your feelings.

And in the practical help and support offered, in the spirit of friendship, to help you get through the weeks to come.

A SPECIAL RELATIONSHIP

Greyfriars Bobby

If you've loved a pet you don't need me to tell you how special the relationship between humans and animals can be.

From the earliest times those close bonds existed. Excavations have revealed human and small dog skeletons buried together, while in Ancient Egypt cats were revered and there were severe penalties for anyone harming them.

Art and literature through the ages tells the same story of unbreakable bonds: as murderous and unlovable as Dickens' Bill Sykes was, he and his dog Bullseye were inseparable.

Who didn't worry along with Dorothy in *The Wizard of Oz* when her nasty neighbour threatened to get Toto taken away? Or shed a tear when Black Beauty finally returned, after many trials, to the country home where he was happiest?

How much more relaxed did Queen Elizabeth II always look out walking her corgis than when attending state occasions? And what visitor to Edinburgh doesn't make the pilgrimage to

Greyfriars Kirkyard to honour the little Skye Terrier, Bobby (pictured left), who kept watch over his master's grave *for fourteen years* until his own death?

It was Immanuel Kant who said "we can judge the heart of a man by his treatment of animals". In return, from our pets we get love and affection, loyalty, fun and fascination, as well as support and service in some cases. No wonder almost half of us choose to share our lives with pets.

Our pets are part of the fabric of our daily lives: picture of
Oli the office cat by Pete Blyth

Chapter 2

When a pet dies

"One of the worst things about Sam dying was not being able to talk to anyone about it. I knew if I said anything at work people would look at me as if I was a bit crazy. I just couldn't explain how huge it was to have lost him. I ended up working from home for a week rather than go in and have people wonder why I couldn't talk to them." **Terry**

Bereavement is a common experience. None of us will go through life without losing someone we care about.

When a friend or relative dies the people we know expect us to be upset. They understand and usually show their sympathy by being kinder and more tolerant if we are distracted or emotional. They ask what they can do to help and tell us they are always on hand to listen.

There are agencies to help us deal with bereavement, and books and services set up to support us. Workplaces have arrangements in place for compassionate leave. There are sections in every card shop where people can choose a beautiful message to tell us they understand our grief and grieve with us.

Many of us experience losing a pet in the same way as we would a human bereavement.

Our animal has been as dear to us as a close, perhaps even a best friend. We may have known it longer than many of the humans in our lives. Certainly we may have spent more time with it. Yet in the case of *pet* loss there are no established routes for navigating our bereavement. We simply don't know where to turn.

Worse, we may fear that some of those closest to us will respond to our grief with bafflement, incomprehension, impatience, even humour – not meant nastily but only adding to this sense that we are somehow alone in our grief, unable to honour or share it.

MIXED EMOTIONS

And why wouldn't other people who haven't experienced losing a pet be baffled when we ourselves hardly understand why our loss is so devastating? Why our emotions are so powerful we scarcely know what to do with them?

We may find we are angry and impatient with ourselves, certain we should be able to better control our feelings. We may get defensive or apologetic that it's taking us so long to 'snap out of it'. Or we may choose to hide away, for fear others will find our obvious distress strange or hard to handle.

It's not unusual to feel guilt or embarrassment alongside the sadness: embarrassment that we are reacting so strongly to the loss of an animal when so many of our fellow humans are suffering so much on a daily basis; guilty that the emotions we're feeling are stronger and more raw than for other bereavements involving a relative or friend.

After all, we know when we take on a pet that it's unlikely to outlive us. We will most likely have to face up to its loss at some point.

I want to reassure you right here and now that whatever you're feeling, however you're experiencing this tremendous loss, you have no need to feel guilty or embarrassed or apologetic.

There are no league tables when it comes to grief and loss. Going through the loss of a beloved animal can be every bit as huge and significant as losing a family member or friend.

We don't grieve in exactly the same way or to precisely the same depth for every friend or relative who dies. Our emotions are in response to what we felt for that person, who they were to us, and, sometimes, the manner of their death.

Why would the loss of a pet be any different?

GROWING RECOGNITION

Increasingly, bereavement and counselling agencies are recognising that how we grieve when we are bereaved depends not on the number of legs or strength of the blood ties, but on what the one we've lost meant to us. And your pet may well have meant the sun, the moon and the stars to you.

Sympathy cards designed for anyone who's lost a much-loved animal have begun to appear in card shops. And a growing number of celebrity memoirs have appeared on bookshelves, describing their love and experience of losing a pet.

Slowly but surely the tide is turning.

"It's been 12 days since that terrible night and everyone thinks I should be back to normal, but how can I be normal when my life is upside down? I hate coming home. I feel as if my heart is broken." **Sandra**

WHY DO WE FEEL SO STRONGLY?

Their love is unconditional

You have every reason to grieve. Our pets are special. Yours was.

If you think about it, for most of us there are only two times in our lives when we are loved unconditionally and without measure. As babies, we come into the world and, hopefully, are greeted with love, delight, indulgence, and full-on attention.

Parents, relatives, friends, neighbours, flock to visit and admire us, tell us how proud they are when we smile or make a sound. It is a heady feeling to be loved and accepted for exactly who we are.

And one we may never entirely experience to the same extent again in our lives – until we have a pet who honours us with the same total, unconditional love and acceptance.

Our pets tolerate our moods, our bad days, bad habits and bad tempers, our foibles and eccentricities and they do not waver in the depth of their love.

Even more than our human partners and close friends – if we are lucky enough to have them – the relationship remains the same from one day to the next, no matter what is going on in the rest of our lives.

Our pets will always be delighted to see us – and will let us know it! They'll be at our side, unchanging, on high days and holidays, through every season, through thick and thin.

That's a huge thing to lose and can leave us feeling as if an anchor has been slashed and we have been cast adrift.

We feel responsible

The comparison with babies is relevant for another reason: whether or not we have experienced parenthood we were all children once and understand how it is to be small and vulnerable; to need the world interpreted for us.

As pet owners, we are very aware of our animals' vulnerability and may see ourselves in a role similar to that of a parent, taking care of them and looking out for them because they are unable to fully understand our 'grown-up' world.

Like babies, they cannot speak to tell us what they fear and what they need and what puzzles them. They depend on us for everything from food and shelter to safety.

That relationship, based on *their* trust, leads to a very special kind of love. Placing their trust in us is one of the biggest gifts anyone or anything can give.

But it is also a responsibility that may, when we lose our pet, lead us to feel that we have let them down in some way – especially if their death was due to accident or illness.

Should we have loved them more? Looked after them more? Protected them more than we did? What a burden such thoughts can be…

They let us be ourselves

With our animal companions we never have to explain ourselves. We never have to be anything other than what and who we are.

You can have a bad hair day or a bad hair life. You can lose your temper with the politicians on tv, mess up at work, say the wrong thing at the wrong time to someone.

You can choose to talk or not talk, to go to bed in the afternoon, spend the day in pyjamas, set the phone to silent, batten down the hatches and make the world go away for a while. Yet you will never find your pet judging you for being yourself, for your successes, failures or foibles.

With your pet you only ever need be yourself.

They are part of the fabric of our daily lives

"I work from home so we were together all the time. I wake up and expect to see her laying by the bed. I take a shower and expect to see her by the bathroom door when I come out. I look under the desk to make sure I won't kick her when I shift my feet. I save scraps from my plate for her. I never realised how much a part she was of every day." **Joanne**

If we are animal lovers the chances are our pets will have been a part – and in some cases the reason – for those life-enhancing moments when we are most relaxed or at peace.

They have become such a part of the fabric of our homes and lives that we cannot imagine a mat without them on it, a garden chair which we don't have to fight them for, waking up in the morning without a soft nose nudging at us to go and sort out some breakfast, or the joyous sound of their greeting as we arrive home - or stroll across the grass to the field where they are kept.

For dog owners the timetable of the day is partly determined by the need to take them out before the day starts and again when it is all over. For horse lovers exercise, grooming, feeding, mucking out, define the shape of their days.

It is hardly surprising that the space they used to occupy now seems so vast and empty. Many of us see more of our pets on a day-to-day basis than most of the people in our lives, however important to us those people might be.

REMEMBER YOU ARE NOT ALONE

If those thoughts on why pet loss can be so profound have struck a chord with you then you must know that you are not alone.

However lost and isolated you might be feeling at this moment, there are millions of others who have loved and lost a cherished animal and know what you are going through.

Over the page, you'll find some suggestions for places to turn to and ways of sharing your feelings and your loss with others who'll understand and may help you through the grieving process.

Burying your feelings may help you get through the day-to-day, especially in the immediate aftermath of your loss, but along with the tears and the huge vacuum of loss if you can possibly find an outlet where you can safely talk about your grief, it will help.

TALK IT OUT

It is almost always helpful to talk but you need to find someone who'll be sympathetic and won't find the depth of your emotion strange. Sometimes help can be found in unexpected places. Any or all of the suggestions below may help you through those first awful days and weeks.

➢ The staff at your local veterinary practice have huge experience in helping pet owners deal with loss, even if a few days or weeks have passed. Don't be scared to contact them and ask what services are available to help you – or simply if you can go into the surgery and talk to someone.

➢ Similarly, your local library or doctor's surgery will be able to put you in touch with the nearest bereavement counselling service in your area if you feel you want professional support.

➢ Trusted friends and family will want to help but sometimes they may be finished with your grief long before you are finished with your need to talk about it. So spread yourself around a bit – you're the only one who knows you've already shared these feelings and your stories ten times already. With each telling you are healing a tiny fraction more, believe me.

➢ You could try sharing your thoughts with other pet owners who will almost always understand. Don't be surprised if you find sympathy in some unlikely quarters: many other people in your acquaintance have never had the chance to open up either.

➢ There are some wonderful pet bereavement helplines – I've listed a few at the end of this book.

➢ Or visit a pet website (addresses for these are also in the Resources section) and post a tribute or join an online chat or support group.

➢ Animal charities – and the charity shops they run - are another place to find like-minded people who will be sympathetic.

➢ But remember, you don't have to explain yourself to anyone if you don't want to. Saying you've suffered a bereavement but feel unable to talk about it is usually enough to stave off enquiries from people who you suspect won't understand.

Lucy and Cindy: picture by Rory Scrivener

Chapter 3

First Aid for Feelings

"It's the day we all dread but the one we know is inevitable. The price we pay for loving someone or something is grief. No matter how much you think you are prepared, how can you possibly be? As a veterinary nurse I have supported many friends and colleagues and the phrase I most often use is 'we never have them long enough'. Our pets are almost transient in our lives, passing through for a short blast. Yet they sometimes make the biggest impact." **Victoria**

In the same way that no two dogs, cats, ponies or guinea pigs are exactly the same, nor is the way we respond to loss.

It's this very fact that we do experience loss so differently from each other – in our own way and our own time – that can make us feel so alone. Yet even as you need to grieve in your own way and to your own timetable, it's useful to know that there are some emotions, and some common stages in bereavement, that many of us who mourn will go through at some point. That way, if they show up you'll be able to recognise them and hopefully draw comfort from some of the thoughts that follow in this chapter.

UNDERSTANDING HOW LOSS WORKS

As you contemplate what you've lost it is useful to remind yourself of a few things.

Firstly, the grief that comes when we lose something or someone we love seems to be experienced cumulatively. Each new loss brings back all the other losses we've lived through.

Whereas with an emotion like anger we may feel it, express it, deal with it, and move on, we seem to struggle to let go of loss completely.

Rather, we learn to live with it, and feel its pain a little less and a little less often over time. But all it takes is some new loss for all that old grief to come flooding back in.

As you mourn the loss of your beloved pet do not be surprised if your feelings seem to re-trigger the grief from other, older losses, disappointments and unhappinesses: from your parents splitting up, redundancy or even children leaving home, to other pets and people you may have lost.

You're not in control of this, nor the strength of your feelings, so instead of resisting, acknowledge whatever comes up, allow yourself to feel whatever you're feeling, and accept your need to mourn – and celebrate - all over again the things you've loved and lost.

And that's the second point to remember. The thing to do with feelings is *feel* them.

We don't choose our feelings. They are the body's way of connecting us to ourselves, cutting through the busyness of daily life to alert us to what is going on within us, and to what we need to pay attention to.

You shouldn't ignore them, any more than you would ignore a warning light flashing on your car dashboard. Both are signals to us that something is amiss and we had better pull over.

If we don't notice and pay attention to those messages it's possible we'll break down.

LOSS IS A ROLLER COASTER

"The early weeks were the most painful for me. By then the shock which helped to numb the pain had worn off. And the sad reality set in. After that my grief came in rolls, like waves on an ocean shore. Sometimes not so bad, other times raging like a storm. I realised all I could do was roll with it." **Zara**

Loss is best described as a roller coaster, hurling our emotions up and down so fast we can feel we have no control over them.

If you've been bereaved before you may already have experienced the uncomfortable highs and lows of loss: raw pain one moment and the next everyone laughing hysterically over some small anecdote at the funeral; an inability to drag yourself from bed, then two hours later you've arranged the whole service and a wake to follow.

These ups and downs are entirely normal. It's as if your skin has been peeled back and every nerve ending feels with an intensity you've not known before.

You think you're beginning to come to terms with your loss then a few moments later find you are in pieces because someone has said a kind word, or because something has reminded you that your pet is no longer there.

Feeling out of control is uncomfortable and stressful and it's tempting to want to try to over-ride the pain by focusing on other things, throwing yourself into work or DIY, or numbing yourself with too many alcoholic drinks or shopping sprees – anything to distract you.

But feelings are nature's way of enabling us to deal with loss and heal from loss. So it's vital not to try and short circuit them – not to jump from the moving roller coaster in other words. Accept that you will have good days, bad days and sometimes awful days and there is often no way of knowing in advance which will be which.

Bottling up your feelings, telling yourself they're unwanted or unacceptable, is a bit like stuffing the cork in a fizzy bottle. In the end they'll almost certainly find another way out – and the resulting explosion could end up hurting you or others even more.

UNDERSTANDING THE STAGES OF LOSS

Remember we are all different so you won't necessarily go through all these stages, or even go through them in this order. But it's helpful to be prepared and to know any of these feelings is quite normal.

Shock and denial – why us?

Whether you knew your pet was dying or would need to be put down, or the death came out of the blue, it's very normal to go through a period of disbelief or denial.

You may not allow yourself to think about it or it may seem as if there are no emotions left in you. You feel numb; as if you're on 'auto-pilot', going through the motions, as though some invisible barrier is separating you from the rest of the world. Everyday life seems all of a sudden to be unreal, and to have nothing to do with you.

Some people experience a false 'high' during this time of being in shock or denial, getting on with things as if nothing has happened, a stranger to themselves and their emotions.

Shock and denial are nature's anesthetic, a way of getting us through those first, awful days of unbelievably raw pain. And if you're a 'coper', the kind who normally deals with everything life throws at you, and likes to be in control, you may be particularly susceptible to slipping into a period of numbness or disbelief.

Life has thrown something entirely unexpected into a life you thought you had under control – and your way of surviving is to mentally deny anything has changed.

If you can't believe it's happened, or can't connect with your feelings, don't add to your load by getting anxious about this response. There really are no rights or wrongs about the way each of us experiences loss.

Trust that nature knows best. Everything happens in its own time and when you are ready to deal with these big emotions you will start to feel them.

Needing to make sense of loss
Along with shock may come the feeling that life is unfair, that bad things ought not to happen to good people and wonderful pets.

You want an explanation, want to understand how this could have happened, and why it happened to you and your beloved animal.

Sometimes we feel that until we are able to understand, to find a reason 'why?', we'll be unable to move on.

In today's world this needing to make sense translates into investigations and public enquiries. The world is such a complicated and often scary place that we feel only through understanding the 'why' – and how to avoid it ever happening again - will we be able to maintain some semblance of control over the chaos.

For you as a pet lover the same principle applies. You don't want your huge loss to be 'senseless' so you allow all those thoughts and questions about 'why', 'how', and 'what if' to chase each other around in your head.

You may also feel you want to know the precise circumstances of your beloved pet's death and that too can be an entirely normal part of coming to terms – just one we tend not to acknowledge because as a society we've tried to airbrush the reality of death out of the picture.

There is nothing sordid or macabre about wanting to know as many details as you can, so long as you recognise that, depending on the circumstances, it may add to your distress. So tread very carefully there, protecting yourself if you need to.

The truth is that sometimes in life there are answers and explanations; and often there are not. Your pet lived very much day-to-day, not regretting the past or anticipating the future, and there's a lesson in that.

It's those who learn to accept that life can be chaotic, random and unfair, but who allow themselves to love and be loved anyway, who find peace the soonest. As with every other stage in your grieving journey, try to treat yourself gently.

Anger and blame

"It was hard enough losing Rusty. I'd had her from a pup. What made it worse was that I blamed Mike for her getting run over. I was away on a course and it was his job to look after her. He knew I thought it was his fault so there was all this guilt and blame and anger between us and we ended up not speaking for several weeks. I can see now that made it even harder. We both loved her so we ought to have been the best people to help each other, instead of which we both retreated into our own worlds."
Marilyn

These feelings of needing to make sense of loss sometimes go along with strong feelings of anger and a need to blame someone: we look for an outlet, somewhere we can vent emotions we fear may overwhelm us.

Perhaps the truth is that someone *was* to blame. That's a really hard thing for you to be facing – and probably for them too.

But before you lash out, do give yourself a chance to feel the fury in private.

Anger is a very physical emotion you see, and it's a good idea to do something physical to express and defuse it before you decide whether you need to take any further action – such as have a conversation with whoever you're angry with.

You could find somewhere private where you can shout and scream or thud a pillow. I find smashing a few plates at the end of the garden, or power walking as if my life depended on it, helps me discharge some of the most intense feelings.

Or you could write an angry letter expressing why you are so furious, then rip it up or burn it without sending.

The same techniques work if you are blindsided by anger, without there being anyone to blame. You're just angry with life, with circumstance, and a world where bad things are allowed to happen.

You will find that bit by bit you feel fractionally better as you allow yourself to unload your anger safely, without harming yourself or those around you.

Sadly, nothing will bring your pet back. If a lesson needs to be learned from what happened, if you need to express something to someone, then, once you've discharged some of the fury in a physical way, make sure it is.

But don't allow yourself to get stuck in blame. Remember that as long as you hang onto blame and anger then it's you who's suffering - carrying the burden of all that emotion on top of everything else.

Guilt

Perhaps you feel you should have loved your pet more, looked after it even more carefully than you did, never got impatient when it wanted food or a walk or just attention and you were busy with something else?

Or perhaps you feel you are somehow to blame for its loss for whatever reason. Along with grieving your pet you are overwhelmed with guilt and can't see how you can forgive yourself.

Guilt is another very common emotion when we are going through loss. It's as if we feel that unless we suffer along with the animal we've lost then we couldn't have loved them enough.

Our guilt is a kind of penance - and yet it is one of the most useless emotions we can get stuck in.

Like worry or anxiety it simply can't change anything or turn back the clock and make things different. It is like fastening a ball and chain to your feet preventing you moving slowly forward through the grieving process.

One thing you can be certain of is that guilt and blame are not feelings your pet would recognise. Remember how your beloved pet hated to see you down in the mouth? How it lived so very much in the moment?

If you are struggling with guilt then allow yourself to gently recognise you don't need to punish yourself any more: you are already suffering so much pain from your loss. While your dear pet can no longer feel pain and definitely wouldn't want you to.

Tell yourself you were doing the best you could at the time with the knowledge, understanding and awareness you had then – because it's true. Hindsight is a wonderful thing but it is not to be trusted. Believe me, if you'd had more awareness or knowledge, if you could have done something differently at the time, you would have.

"Some animals – especially rabbits and ruminants such as sheep or goats – are extremely stoic. We only really know something is wrong when it's too late, then find we're blaming ourselves for not noticing sooner." **Sally**

The pit
As I said, we rarely experience feelings of loss and grief in a 'straight line'.

Just when you think you might be able to look at a picture of your pet again without crying you stumble on an empty pet bowl in the cupboard and start to howl.

You can hardly believe that after all this time and all these tears the grief seems as real and as strong as ever.

Yet once you've dried your eyes you may be able to take a step back and acknowledge that it's taken you a little less time to recover than it did during the first few days of your loss. Slowly, very slowly, time is taking the raw edge from your grief.

The exception to this is when grief subsides into a kind of permanent heavy-heartedness, as if the world has turned grey: you wonder in the mornings what there is to get out of bed for and each day passes you by without you really being a part of it. It feels as if you are alone on one side of a screen, going through the motions, disconnected from everything in your life.

Life has become a kind of flatline.

If this happens to you, and you realise that there are no signs you're beginning to move through grief, then your loss may have triggered depression and it would be sensible to seek professional help from your doctor. Our minds and bodies are brilliant but complex instruments and there is nothing to be ashamed of or afraid of in asking for help.

Far from being weak, it is the strong who recognise they need help and find enough courage to ask for it.

Acceptance

I'm including acceptance in this short introduction to the stages of grief because, as hard as it is to believe right now, at some stage you will find you are no longer resisting what has happened; you'll be able to acknowledge you have suffered a bereavement and realise somehow you will survive it.

Reaching this point doesn't mean you've stopped feeling sad, but the huge extremes of emotion that overwhelmed you at first will level out a little until they cease to hijack you as dramatically as they did at the start.

You won't be thinking about your loss all the time and not everything will remind you of your missing pet. Perhaps memories of some of the happy times you shared will begin to come more frequently to mind in place of those early vivid pictures of loss and pain.

It's important to tell yourself that reaching the stage where you accept your loss is not a betrayal of your pet. Pets bring us such joy, and they love to see us happy and share our happiness with us. As I've already reminded you, our grief upsets them.

Giving and receiving love is the greatest gift this planet has to offer us and you experienced that with your wonderful and unique animal.

In time you'll want to celebrate what you brought to your pet's life, and what he or she brought to yours.

Sonny in the sink: picture by Viv

Chapter 4

Living through loss

"It is easier to believe that we are always responsible ("if only I had done/not done this one thing") than it is to accept this painful truth: we are not in control of the world. Stuff happens. Bad stuff. As brilliant and responsible and hard-working and control-freaky that we are, sometimes, bad stuff just happens." **Patricia B McConnell**

As I pointed out in the last chapter, there are no short cuts when it comes to grieving someone or something we have loved and lost.

A common experience is just wanting the hurt to go away, to fast-forward to some future point where it just isn't so painful to think of your lost pet.

The truth is that the best way out, indeed the only way out, is *through*. But there are things you can do and tools you can use to help you navigate that 'through'.

STOP THE CLOCKS

In the last chapter I urged you to feel your feelings rather than suppress them. And in the immediate days of loss the best thing you can do is cancel everything and stay at home, looking after yourself and honouring your grief and whatever emotions you are feeling.

Despite what anyone might say about 'life goes on', it doesn't have to. In the early days why shouldn't you allow life to stop in order to be with your grief?

Once upon a time society recognised this through the tradition of mourning. Some cultures had a set period for this, giving everyone a chance to step off the hurly-burly of life for a period.

Nowadays, in our fast-moving world, the idea of taking time out seems strange, even self-indulgent. Yet our ancestors knew better than us that grief and loss need time and space and sometimes the quiet of our own company until we are ready to step back into the world.

TIMETABLE YOUR GRIEVING

A week or two in you may want to consider giving yourself a break from this round-the-clock pain by scheduling in times when you can be busy and distracted alongside quieter times when you can return to your grieving process.

There are all kinds of ways in which you can give yourself a break from all that raw emotion, from heading to the cinema to immerse yourself in a film for two hours, to throwing yourself into work, seeking out the kind of company where you wouldn't dream of talking about your loss, or starting some kind of project.

The important thing is that whatever you choose to do, it's something that requires your full concentration. You'll still be aware of a weight, a deep sadness, underneath the surface, but keeping active will hold the strong emotions at bay until you switch back into some quiet time for you and your thoughts and feelings about your loss.

It's all about balance: giving yourself permission to close your mind to your loss for a little while each day, but returning to it when you can be private and gentle with yourself.

PRACTICE SELF-CARE

Most of us aren't brilliant at this. We're brought up believing that to put ourselves and our needs first is selfish.

In my experience, no-one who worries that looking after themselves during difficult times may be selfish is in any danger of being so. Self-care is no more than caring for ourselves as we do for others, redirecting the compassion and understanding we so often give out *inwards* for a while.

And if there is ever a time to put your own feelings and needs first it's when you are bereaved.

Practicing self-care might mean saying 'no' to things you don't want to do, or requests people make, more often than you usually do.

If you're someone who has a lot of commitments and is constantly busy it might mean slowing down for a while and not trying to meet your own high expectations of yourself.

It might mean allowing yourself to tune in more often than you do to what your body is telling you it needs: switching off the alarm and allowing yourself to sleep late, for instance, or adapting your daily routine to make time for long therapeutic walks, meeting up with friends you don't see enough, or hunkering down with a good book and a mug of cocoa In fact anything that brings you a little peace or a sense that you are nurturing yourself.

It means treating yourself with the same love and care you gave your beloved pet: that means sympathy, tenderness and attention. No beating yourself up or pushing yourself to 'shape up'.

REMIND YOURSELF OFTEN THAT TIME DOES HELP

Remember that sooner or later – however impossible it seems– time will begin its healing process.

That doesn't mean you won't still be sad sometimes when you think about your pet and the wonderful times you shared together.

Clichés become clichés because they are true for most of us: time may not fix things and it can't undo the past. But it does help us heal at an emotional level as surely as your body eventually repairs a physical wound.

Your pain won't be as intense as this forever. Think back to other times in your life when you were really unhappy, perhaps as a child when someone hurt you or you were really anxious about something.

Now you look back, you can see your feelings are no longer so strong. They've passed and you've survived and learned and grown a little.

Emotional hurts may not be visible to us in the way a wound is but it's useful to think about them in the same way: treat your hurt as you might an injury, with care and kindness, and with patience, knowing that if you do so your body will begin to mend itself.

The wounds that don't heal and become troublesome are the ones that are ignored.

"I think we all want to be loved and remembered when we die, but we also want to know that the ones we left behind are doing alright without us – because we love them so much. Now I can see that because my pet loved me so much, being strong is one of the ways I can return that." **Jonathan**

THIS HELPED ME HEAL

"I started a habit of imagining myself in my pet's place. If I had died, how would I want him to be? I wouldn't want him to be unhappy but to go on enjoying the walks and the comfort of home and the excitement of new faces and places. Then I tell myself of course he'd want the same for me – and it's true!"
Simone

"I learned who I could be with and who I could talk to – and who I couldn't. There were some people in my life who couldn't cope with my grief. I felt like they were trying to hurry me through it by not talking about it; talking about everything but really. In the end there were just two friends I felt safe sharing with and it was them who got me through."
Alison

"I wrote. Pages and pages, about how I was feeling. About how desperate I was. All my anger and all the tears, just poured onto the page. I did it every morning, sometimes more than once, and in the end I was needing to do it less. It really helped."
Angela

"Someone told me that exercise helped them. So I joined the local gym and they were right. Something about working up a sweat, pounding the treadmill, pushing weights, did give me an outlet for what I was feeling. I'm still a member!"
Paul

"I bought the prettiest but toughest plant I could find. This gave me something to look after and care for – nowhere near filling the gap, but I couldn't bear the thought of going home and having nothing to care for and keep happy. To this day I am careful about keeping this

plant alive – it helps me feel a part of her has lived on, especially when 'her' flowers bloom."

Sally

"A few weeks after my dog died a friend was trying to rehome her mum's dog. Her mum had died and she said the dog was as bereft as everyone else. I worried it was too soon to take on another pet but actually Alfie helped me heal. He seemed to sense I was grieving too and let me cry into his coat. It was as if my old dog sent Alfie to me."

Sarah

Rachel sharing a cuddle with Gizmo:
picture by Nathan Spellman

Chapter 5

Children and bereavement

"My mum always said children losing a pet is a good lesson for when the 'biggies' go and I definitely agree with that, though I have felt a greater grief losing some of my pets than some family members." **Victoria**

Children react to the death of a pet in many different ways, depending on their age and what else may be going on in their lives.

If they are already struggling, perhaps with school or friendships, fitting in, or family relationships, the loss of a pet's unconditional love and approval can trigger some powerful emotions.

Particularly if you are aware of difficulties for them at school or in their friendships, do speak to their teachers about what has happened so that your child can be supported when they are away from home as well as when they are with you.

For young children the loss of a pet may be their first experience of death and on top of missing your beloved animal they will be grappling with fear about this discovery that animals, people and things we love can simply vanish from their lives: permanent and reliable one day; gone the next.

They may have lots of questions and even though you are grieving it's important to give children the space and permission to talk about their feelings – and to answer their questions as honestly as possible without going into distressing details.

There are some excellent books now available to help youngsters understand some of these major life experiences and see that other children go through them too. They are not alone, any more than you are. Check your local library or ask in a bookshop to be directed to the area where they keep books written to help children through tough times.

You can also help them by allowing them to be involved in whatever arrangements you make for your beloved pet's burial or cremation, and their commemoration. Giving them the chance to express their wishes, help make choices, and play a role in any ceremony you may decide to organise, is a way of letting them know you recognise their feelings and need to grieve too – as well as the role your pet played in their lives.

If your children are older, in their teens or even beyond, that doesn't mean they won't also be grieving, perhaps just as intensely as you. Life is often already pretty challenging and confusing for young people. They have a huge amount on their plates but not necessarily the life skills to deal with an onslaught of emotion, or the ability to express their feelings aloud.

Pets are a part of the package they identify as 'home'. And in a world that often moves too fast for them, and where so many things are uncertain, home is a foundation stone they subconsciously rely on to keep them at least a little anchored through the stress of study, exams or careers, first relationships and relationship breakdown, fears about the future and fragile self-esteem, plus the permanently-on pressures of social media.

The same applies even if your adult children have moved away from home. Suddenly, through the death of a much-loved pet who has always been there, home has changed. Something they had counted on to stay the same has shifted.

Of course you'll want to offer them the opportunity to share their feelings with you for as long as they need to. Maybe they will, sometimes they won't or can't. And you certainly can't force it if that's the case.

If this happens you can still be there for them and reassure them that their grief is seen and understood – and it's ok.

For instance you can send daily supportive messages to their phones, letting them know it's ok to grieve, telling them you're hurting for them and that you'll support them in any way you can. Reassuring them you're standing by if they need any help.

Tell them the things I've told you: that our love for our animals can be as strong as our love for family members or friends. And how important a part of your pet's life they were.

You can also try talking a little about your own grief, not in the expectation that they will comfort you but as a prompt for them, if they want it, to open up a fraction too.

But let me say again, at the end of this section, that there are no rights and wrongs when it comes to children and loss.

It's quite possible – especially with young children – that their sadness will arrive like a storm and then depart the next day as suddenly as it arrived. Or it may never arrive at all. Some children are not deeply involved with their pets, or may appear more curious than upset.

Be prepared for their reaction to take whatever course it does, with no expectations but simply compassion and under-standing for as long as it's needed.

Smudge, Sally's much-loved and missed bunny

Chapter 6

The greatest love –
having your pet put down

*"I could not watch him suffer any more as I knew he was
suffering for me. Putting him to sleep was the most difficult
decision I've ever had to make and I've questioned my decision
over and over again. Is there something more I could have done?
Should I have kept trying? I know I did the right thing for him,
but it feels so wrong. I just have to find comfort in knowing he is
no longer suffering." **Beth***

It may be that you have picked up this book because you are
facing one of the toughest decisions we can be asked to make:
whether to have your pet put to sleep.

What makes it tough is not only anticipating such a huge loss, but
the confusion of knowing when is the right time to make the
decision.

You love your pet: it's absolutely natural that you want to do
everything in your power to help them if there is a chance they
can get well again or at least have a good quality of life during a
prolonged illness.

And yet there will come a time when your vet, your pet through its behaviour, or your own instincts, tell you it is time to let go.

You need to know that giving permission for your pet to be put to sleep is not a failure on your part but an act of huge compassion and courage.

You are putting its peace of mind, its need to move to the next stage in the circle of life, ahead of your own need to be with your pet.

Euthanasia actually means 'gentle death'.

When that moment comes think hard about what you need to do to make such a difficult time as easy on you both as possible in the circumstances.

Perhaps you want the vet to come to you? Perhaps you want it to be a time when you know you can take a few days to recover, for instance at the end of the week or when you have few commitments?

Is your pet likely to be more alarmed by a stranger coming into the house than being taken to the surgery that they may be used to?

If your pet is already at the surgery is it kinder to leave it there or bring it home? If the operation is performed at the surgery is there someone who can come and support you?

Can the vet give you time alone with your pet afterwards?

Do you need someone to drive you home in private?

WHEN TO LET GO

Is your pet:

- ➢ Suffering from pain, distress or serious discomfort which can't be controlled with medication?

- ➢ Having difficulty walking or balancing?

- ➢ Finding it difficult to eat and drink enough without vomiting?

- ➢ Suffering from tumours which cause pain and are inoperable or untreatable?

- ➢ Having difficulty breathing?

- ➢ Incontinent or having difficulty urinating or defecating?

- ➢ Behaving in ways that are totally out of character?

If you've answered yes to any of these the time may have come to consider whether you need to let go.

I know a lot of people feel guilty about having their pets euthanised but they should think how they might feel if they hadn't. I'm still haunted by the memory of how ill Sky was before I called the vet out to him and if I could change things now I think I would have called the vet earlier, although I really did what I thought was best for him at the time." **Yvonne**

WHAT HAPPENS WHEN YOUR PET IS PUT DOWN?

If you are going to the surgery do explain when you make the appointment that you are having your pet put to sleep so they can give you a longer appointment – and time with your beloved animal afterwards.

It may be wise to ask for the last appointment of the day when there are fewer people around and no-one to be held up.

Consider asking if you can pay in advance or someone else can settle your bill. The staff won't want to trouble you afterwards when you are in the first waves of grief, any more than you'll want to stop and do the paperwork.

You might want to take something familiar with you, like your pet's bed or a favourite toy. And if you're planning to bring them home afterwards, then remember to pack a blanket.

Sometimes the vet may use a sedative first to calm your pet, before giving the injection. This will help it start to feel sleepy and reduce the chances of there being any distress when the second injection goes into a vein. But if it's already calm, or perhaps its condition means it is not active, then the vet may go straight to the euthanasia.

Remember, as its carer, you know your pet better than anyone and if you have views on what would suit it best then do speak up.

The drug used to put your animal to sleep is similar to an anesthetic and if you've ever had one you'll know that it works quickly and peacefully. It won't take long for them to slip away and they won't be in any pain.

Some pet owners find staying in the room too painful and there's no failure in acknowledging that if it's the case for you. If you're distressed your animal may well sense that. But if you are able to stay with your pet then you can be a part of giving it 'a good death', offering familiarity, reassurance and deep love, by talking gently and stroking them as they move to their next chapter…

FOR HORSE OWNERS

According to World Horse Welfare, only one in eight horses die from natural causes, which means the majority of those who keep horses or ponies will face the difficult choice of having to have their animal put down.

The same organisation, whose details you'll find in the resources section at the end of this book, offers a couple of excellent 'just in 'case' leaflets, giving you invaluable information about what's involved, the choices you face, and making a plan long before it is needed.

There are two options for horse owners to consider: injection or a 'bolt' or 'shot' to the head. This sounds horrific but in some circumstances may be kinder. Horses are flight animals so in certain cases their response to the injection may be to try and run from danger. Knowing your horse well will enable you to know what is best for them.

Think carefully about whether it is right for you to be there. If you are obviously upset will your horse pick up on that? Is there a trusted friend who can hold your horse, or can the vet arrange to have someone to do that?

If you do choose to be there at the end make sure you've prepared by reading the World Horse Welfare information on what to expect.

The other preparation to make is what happens to your much-loved animal once he or she has been put to sleep. At such a distressing time you don't want the added stress of needing to research options that may include burial on your land (if you have space and you'll need local authority permission to do so), the fallen stock collectors (also known as 'knackers') or a local abbatoir.

Like vets, these people are experts are what they do and will be understanding and professional with you and your horse.

As distressing as it may be to consider all these practical details, remind yourself that euthanasia is an act of love on your part.

VIEW FROM THE OTHER SIDE

Victoria Beasley of the Minster Veterinary Practice shares some thoughts from the other side of the counter.

"As you can imagine, my professional life is filled with the loss of pets, the majority being euthanased. Euthanasia puts a very different spin on death and in turn the grief. It's a decision to wrestle with as there is no going back and I know people struggle with guilt afterwards.

As the Veterinary Oath says, we must not let an animal in our care suffer. I never mind being asked to assist and even after 20 years of doing so I still find it sad — we often shed a tear afterwards or sometimes with the owner if we have been particularly involved with that patient. I don't think it's unprofessional to do that. I think it says a lot about us and why we do what we do.

Clients often say "you must hate this". I want to say 'no' without sounding weird. For me, making sure a euthanasia 'goes well' and the pet isn't distressed or in pain, and that it's peaceful, is really important. These are the final moments of a pet's life and for both the owner and the pet I want that to go well. It's almost a privilege to assist with that, particularly if you have been invited into someone's home to do it.

I would urge owners to stay if they can bear it. Everything our pets have to face is easier with their human by their side and they often 'look' for their owners."

Harley: picture by Jools Bennett

Chapter 7

Living with uncertainty:
when a pet goes missing

"It was not knowing where she was that was the hardest. I honestly think finding out she was dead would have been easier than waking every day with this black cloud, worrying she was lying somewhere injured or locked in or had been hurt in some way. For weeks afterwards I couldn't settle to anything. It still hurts." **Ellen**

One of the cruellest fates that can befall any animal lover is to have their pet disappear.

We imagine the worst and long for the best. We scour the neighbourhood, put out appeals wherever we can, stalk social media for news, call every vet in the area, stick up signs, hammer on shed doors, leave the litter tray or blanket outside, trek in dread along the roadsides... and hope. My goodness, how we hope.

But as each day passes and there is no sign of our beloved animal, no news, hope turns to despair. Like Ellen, we'd rather know the worst, so we can begin to grieve, than to feel this weight of pessimism, anxiety and despair.

So long as there is no news, no sign, no body, we are left hanging in a kind of limbo, unable to start mourning but equally unable to get on with anything else.

It is absolutely normal at such times to experience all the same stages of loss – guilt, anger, grief – but added to them may be an inability to concentrate, feelings of being lost or stuck, or a sense of everything else in your life being on hold.

You're likely to be beside yourself with anxiety too, and fear for what your pet may be going through. One of the things that causes us most stress in our lives is feeling out of control of a situation. And now the days turn into weeks that's exactly how it seems: as if your fate is out of your own hands.

As much as you can, be gentle with your own thoughts. Our imaginations almost always conjure up far worse scenarios than real life. We are all good at terrifying ourselves with our thinking, even though experts say that 95% of what we worry about or conjure in our minds never happens.

This is a time to distract yourself and refuse to give head room to your imagination.

I want to say don't give up too soon. Miracles happen. Our animals do find their way home to us. They do turn up bedraggled and skinny from some adventure we can only guess at. Our lovely

Pocket once went missing for ten days and we were beside ourselves until the morning we came downstairs to find her waiting once more at the kitchen door.

My friend Sarah's cat was missing a similar time and she too turned the neighbourhood upside down before one evening, when it was quiet, she heard a scuffling under the floorboards. Somehow her aged cat had found a way through a tiny hole left by the plumber. Sarah couldn't understand why she hadn't responded to all the calling. But we know that while some animals react noisily to fear, others may hunker down into the tightest corner and stay as small and quiet as they can.

I hope with all my heart you and your beloved pet have a happy ending.

But you can only deal with living in limbo for so long; sooner or later, if your pet does not come home, you need to give yourself permission to accept they have gone – in order that you can begin the grieving process.

That may mean linking up with others who've experienced a pet's disappearance by contacting one of the places listed in the resources section. They will know exactly what you are going through.

Or share your feelings of pain and uncertainty with family or friends that you trust – or staff at your local veterinary surgery. Don't feel as if you can't because you don't know whether your pet is alive or dead: it's you they care about and they'll want to support you through this difficult time.

The lovely Pringle: another great picture by Jools Bennett

Chapter 8

Thoughts on practicalities

"It was the children who asked if we were going to have a funeral and even though it was emotional it helped me as well as them. I let them arrange everything and I suppose afterwards there was a feeling of relief, of lightness." **Jenny**

By the time you read this you may already have made the decision about whether your beloved pet is to be buried or cremated, whether the ashes are to be returned, or not.

You don't usually need permission to bury your pet in your garden – if you own your house – but it can be a hard thing to do, bringing home the reality of your loss.

For that reason, many people now choose cremation.

There are pet crematoria in every region and all local vets will be able to direct you to the nearest one, or arrange the cremation for you. Make sure you ask about your choices: there are crematoria that are part of an established chain and smaller independent operations. .

You will be asked whether you want an individual cremation – so that your pet's ashes can be returned to you. Or a simple communal cremation, which will mean the ashes can't be returned.

If you opt for individual cremation you will be asked which casket you want – your choices will range from a simple cardboard box to carved and decorated wooden caskets – or baskets in the case of horses and other larger animals.

It's then up to you to choose whether you want to keep the casket, either for burial somewhere in your own garden or to keep in your home. Cat lover to the end, my uncle kept the ashes from all six of the pets he'd adored through his lifetime – so that when the time came their ashes could be scattered alongside his own.

Alternatively, you can ask for the casket to be buried at the crematorium or in a pet cemetery. Most crematoria have Books of Remembrance where your much-loved and missed animal can be commemorated.

COMMEMORATE AND CELEBRATE YOUR PET
Whatever you decide, you may well feel you want to do something more to mark your loss, and to celebrate the dear friend your pet was to you.

There's no need to be embarrassed about that. For centuries those who could afford it set up little pet cemeteries close to their homes. There's scarcely a stately home without its own pet graveyard.

In our day and age, as we've come to recognise the importance of our pets in our lives, a number of companies have begun to offer pet memorials of every style and price – from a simple memorial note on a pet lover's website to a full-blown granite headstone.

The important thing to remember is that making arrangements to commemorate your pet is actually far more about you than about them. Thinking and planning how we want to celebrate our pets keeps us busy and gives us a focus and outlet for the myriad of emotions we are experiencing.

It's a way of keeping us occupied during the first awful days of grief, without having to pretend nothing has happened.

In exactly the same way that preparing a funeral for a friend or relative helps us gather our thoughts, remember what they meant to us, and allows us to feel we are carrying out a final act of caring, so too does making those same arrangements for our pet.

We are demonstrating what they meant to us and performing an act of service to show our gratitude to them for all that they contributed to our lives.

So be sure to make choices that feel right to you rather than worrying about doing things in the way you think they 'ought' to be done.

FUNERAL FOR A FRIEND

Unlike traditional funerals, your pet funeral can take any form you like. It may be no more than a short prayer or reading a poem at the bottom of the garden. Or you may want to invite friends who knew and loved your pet too.

You may want to organise music, a tribute, readings – or all of those things.

It can be nice to ask those who knew your pet well to write down or read out a memory of a time you all shared, and for you to do the same. Whether or not you use them in some kind of ceremony, you can certainly collect them together in a small album, together with photos and your own memories.

If you struggle to express your feelings in words, find a poem or song that resonates with you. At the end of this book are a few suggestions for poems and readings.

You can also find plenty of poetry and suitable reflections on some of the websites listed in the resources section.

You might even like to write your own.

MUSIC FOR REMEMBERING

You will have your own favourites – and it's possible your pet did too! But, if not, here are some suggestions you may like:

- ➤ The Circle of Life from The Lion King (Elton John)
- ➤ Let it Be (The Beatles)
- ➤ Over the Rainbow (Judy Garland and many others!)
- ➤ Fields of Gold (Eva Cassidy)
- ➤ Fly (Celine Dion)
- ➤ Bright Eyes (Art Garfunkel)
- ➤ Time to Say Goodbye (Katherine Jenkins and others)
- ➤ You'll be in my Heart (Phil Collins)
- ➤ Tears in Heaven (Eric Clapton)
- ➤ Somewhere Only We Know (Lilly Allen)
- ➤ Angel (Sarah McLachlan)
- ➤ Bring me Sunshine (Morecambe and Wise)

A PLACE TO REMEMBER

You may want your pet's body, ashes or memorial close by in the garden, or, if you don't have space, somewhere your pet loved to go: a favourite haunt or walk that you both enjoyed visiting.

Alternatively, most crematoria have a garden of remembrance where you can place a memorial, or a book of remembrance where you can write your thoughts or include a photograph.

The advantage of erecting a stone or creating a special place for your pet is that you have somewhere real where you can go and remember.

You may not feel the need for that: many people say they can sense their pet in and around the home the way they always were.

But it can be consoling to create a special place of remembrance, for instance by planting a rose tree or other shrub or flower, erecting a stone, or perhaps a bench or seat where you can sit and feel grateful to have had your pet's love.

Many vets surgeries keep noticeboards for pictures of pets, or their own book of remembrance where you can write down your thoughts or a special tribute.

If your local surgery doesn't have a book yet try suggesting the idea to them – you'll be doing a service to other pet owners.

A PERMANENT TRIBUTE TO YOUR PET

There are plenty of other – very practical - ways to pay tribute to your pet, which may also benefit other animals. For example:

- ➢ sponsor an animal at a rescue centre, zoo or charity such as The Blue Cross

- ➢ make a donation to an animal charity or get involved with their activities

- ➢ organise a sponsored event to support a relevant charity

- ➢ volunteer some time to help at an animal sanctuary

- ➢ create a scrapbook of photos and memories

- ➢ commission a painting from a photograph of your pet

- ➢ name a star for your little star!

- ➢ post a tribute to them on one of the pet memory websites.

And don't overlook the obvious – a favourite picture for the wall, which will remind you of the fun and love you shared; and give you the chance to tell stories and remember what made your pet such an individual.

Why stop at one animal? Emmi and Benni with Bob

Chapter 9

Life after loss

"I still get sad when I think about him not being here any more. But it's getting easier to remember the things about him that made me smile, his face at the window as if he knew I was coming home, the warm lump on my bed, the way he had of staring at me as if he was willing me to get up and feed him again." **Paul**

The sadness of your loss may never leave you completely but, in time, the pain of it will lessen.

You may only think about your pet from time to time, when a word or object or place reminds you of the missing face in your life. Though the memories that come to mind may be bitter-sweet, increasingly you may find yourself smiling at some of the happier memories of times you shared together.

If this doesn't happen and, after a few months, you still find yourself often in tears then you may need to seek professional help, either from a counselling agency or a special bereavement service – see the resources section for suggestions.

As the pain fades from the almost unbearable to an occasional heartache, there is no need to feel guilty about this.

Your pet loved to see you happy.

As humans we don't keep animals to add to our load but to enjoy and cherish. You did not take on your beloved pet on in order to feel sad but to love and be loved and you can continue to do that even though your pet is out of sight.

NO REPLACEMENT

One of the first things people will ask you, or suggest to you, is that you should get another animal.

But keeping a pet is not like replacing a light bulb. You need time to grieve, time to adjust, and time to assess, before you consider whether to take such a significant step.

It's quite normal to feel for a while that you never want to put yourself in the position again where you may lose something you love. But, trust me on this, such feelings usually pass over time.

One of the wonderful things about the human heart is that there is no limit on the love it can contain. Just because you are ready to love another pet takes nothing from the love you feel for the pet you lost.

We have an endless capacity to love: just ask anyone who keeps six, sixteen or sixty animals!

Sometimes we feel guilty all over again, as if getting another pet is in some way a betrayal of the pet we lost.

In reality it's the opposite. It's precisely because we loved our pet so much – and got so much back – that we want to do it all over again.

And just think what joy you bring to an animal's life.

Your love is a gift to your pet, as surely as your pet brings pleasure and love to your life.

"I feel sad if people say they can't face having another pet. Where does all the love go that you gave to your pet? I encourage people to let time heal and consider giving that love to another. They adore you and who wouldn't want that?"
Victoria

THE ROAD AHEAD

In the days and weeks to come may you draw strength from remembering the pleasure, comfort and love you and your beloved pet did share.

May you want to share with the rest of us stories of the very special relationship that exists between us and the animals we love.

May you heal and be whole again, knowing that is how your beloved animal wanted you to be.

And may you draw comfort from our miraculous capacity to go on loving, even when we cannot see or be with the object of that love.

"What the heart has once known, it shall never forget." Anon

Chapter 10
Further resources

WEBSITES AND OTHER ORGANISATIONS THAT CAN HELP

Do note that the internet is full of resources that may help you – with more sites being added all the time. This list is only a small selection of those that I, or other pet lovers, have found useful. Please tell me of any others you find so that I can add them to future editions - or indeed of any updates to this information.

Blue Cross
www.bluecross.org.uk
support line: 0800 096 6606
The Blue Cross runs a pet bereavement support service via telephone or email. You'll be able to talk to a trained volunteer befriender who will understand what you are going through.

Chances Spot
www.chancesspot.org
Chances spot offers forums, pet grief and bereavement hotlines, helpful information, resources for children, and a space to commemorate your beloved pet.

Friends at the End
www.bhs.org.uk/welfare-and-care/our-work/our-campaigns/friends-at-the-end
support line: 02476 840517
Friends at the End is a part of the British Horse Society, offering advice and support through bereavement for horse owners.

Cats Protection

www.cats.org.uk/what-we-do/grief-and-loss

Paws to Listen Grief Support Service: 0800 024 94 94

A range of expert resources including a 'pet wall' for your pet's photo.

World Horse Welfare

www.worldhorsewelfare.org

helpline: 0800 480 180

The Ralph Site

www.theralphsite.com

A wide range of resources to help people through pet loss, including counsellors specialising in animal bereavement.

EASE

https://ease-animals.org.uk/pet-loss-support

A series of podcasts and downloadable resources on topics around pet loss, such as guilt, supporting a friend, and helping children commemorate their animal.

Pet loss

www.petloss.com

This US website carries tributes, poems and stories from those whose pets have died; visitors are encouraged to add their own and to take part in a global Monday evening candle ceremony to remember pets. There's also a chat room, links to other useful websites, and relevant articles.

POETRY AND READINGS

The readings and poems in this section are from a range of sources and are offered simply as suggestions or starting points as you make your own choices, depending on your own beliefs and circumstances.

Rainbow Bridge

Just this side of heaven is a place called Rainbow Bridge.

When an animal dies that has been especially close to someone here, that pet goes to Rainbow Bridge.

There are meadows and hills for all of our special friends so they can run and play together.

There is plenty of food, water and sunshine, and our friends are warm and comfortable.

All the animals who had been ill and old are restored to health; those who were hurt or maimed are made whole and strong, just as we remember them in our dreams of days and times gone by.

The animals are happy and content, except for one small thing; they each miss someone very special to them, who had to be left behind.

They all run and play together, but the day comes when one suddenly stops and looks into the distance.

His bright eyes are intent; his eager body quivers.

Suddenly he begins to run from the group, flying over the green grass, his legs carrying him faster and faster.

You have been spotted, and when you and your special friend finally meet, you cling together in joyous reunion, never to be parted again.

The happy kisses rain upon your face; your hands again caress the beloved head, and you look once more into the trusting eyes of your pet, so long gone from your life but never absent from your heart.

Then you cross the Rainbow Bridge together....

Author unknown

***Extract from* Ecclesiastes 3.1-8**
To everything there is a season, and a time to every purpose under the heaven: a time to be born and a time to die; a time to plant, and a time to pluck up that which is planted...a time to weep and a time to laugh; a time to mourn and a time to dance.

Do not stand at my grave
Do not stand at my grave and weep
I am not there. I do not sleep.
I am a thousand winds that blow.
I am the diamond glints on snow.
I am the sunlight on ripened grain.
I am the gentle autumn rain.
When you awaken in the morning's hush
I am the swift uplifting rush
Of quiet birds in circled flight.
I am the soft stars that shine at night.
Do not stand at my grave and cry;
I am not there. I did not die.
Mary Elizabeth Frye

What is Dying?
A ship sails and I stand watching
'til she fades on the horizon, and
someone at my side says, "She is gone".
Gone where?

Gone from my sight, that is all.
The diminished size and total loss of
Sight is in me…and just at
The moment when someone at my side says
"She is gone," there are others who are
watching her coming,
And other voices
Take up a glad shout, "There she comes!"
And that is dying.
Bishop Brent

Something beautiful
The tide recedes, but leaves behind bright seashells on the sand.
The sun goes down but gentle warmth still lingers on the land.
The music stops, and yet it echoes on in sweet refrains.
For every joy that passes, something beautiful remains.
Author unknown

In Blackwater Woods
…To live in this world
you must be able
to do three things:
to love what is mortal;
to hold it
against your bones knowing
your own life depends on it;
and, when the time comes to let it go,
to let it go
From In Blackwater Woods by Mary Oliver

Another furry member of the family gone from our sight: Amy with Twiglet

Acknowledgements

Many thanks to Paul Manning of Astonlee Veterinary Surgery, Newport Pagnell, who not only cast an expert eye over the first edition of this book but shared some useful insights from his own practice. Thanks, too, to Victoria Beasley of The Minster Veterinary Practice in York for some invaluable suggestions for this new edition.

The Animal Health Centre in Bristol have been supportive for many years, as has Kevin Spurgeon of the Association of Private Pet Crematoria and Cemeteries - who also offered important feedback and advice. For this new edition, Ally Todd-McCabe of the brilliant Trusted Friends Pet Crematorium, Milton Keynes, expertly reviewed the text – and was the very definition of compassion when she handled the collection and cremation of our dear cat Twiglet.

I am grateful to Yvonne Cook for her useful suggestions, for gentle editing, and for sharing her own experience of losing a pet. Sally Cottingham did the same and I am especially grateful to her for improving the scope of this book through the information she shared on loving and losing horses and rabbits.

Thanks to those who generously allowed me to use their photos – and to all of those who also sent pictures I was unable to use. I wish I'd been able to include more. The list includes Amy, Bev, Bob, Gill, Henk, Jane, Nathan, Olga, Pete, Robyn, Sally, Shushie, Tracy, Victoria, Viv, and Jools (of <u>bespokehousesitters.co.uk</u>). My nephew Rory gets a special mention here because he runs a photography business: <u>roryscrivener.co.uk</u>. A special mention too to the photographer behind the superb cover photo, Timmy_L (see the full credit on p.4). Huge thanks to Caroline Jarrett for working her magic to transform it into a usable cover. The quote on p.45 from Patricia B McConnell came from her excellent blog – now also a book I believe – *The Other End of the Leash.*

Above all, the book could not have been written without input from the many pet owners who shared their memories and thoughts – in the hope they would help others. More than a decade since the first edition appeared, I would like to think *Losing A Pet* will continue for many years supporting anyone experiencing the death or disappearance of a much-loved pet. With that in mind I'd like to invite you to contact me if you have experiences – or indeed photos – to share for future editions. You can find my contact details at **www.janematthews.com**

Printed in Poland
by Amazon Fulfillment
Poland Sp. z o.o., Wrocław